Zombie Apocalypse Survival Handbook

Staying Alive in the Land of the Living Dead

By Ivan So

Introduction

I want to thank you and for downloading the book, *Zombie Apocalypse Survival Handbook: Staying Alive in the Land of the Living Dead*.

This book contains proven steps and strategies on how to survive a zombie apocalypse.

The threat of an apocalypse dominated by the living dead is a very real scenario. This book discusses evidence of zombie existence throughout history, and the lingering possibilities of pathogens that could destroy all of humankind. Currently, there are two ongoing cases of zombie infections, and this book dissects those instances in order to better prepare you for the inevitability that one of those viruses will lead to the doom of humanity. You must take immediate action and respond properly in order to survive, and reading this handbook is the first step you must take.

By the time you finish this book, you will know how to persevere yourself through the initial zombie pandemic, and then, how to fight and defeat any zombies that cross your path as the world falls apart around you. You will learn where to find shelter, food, water, and weaponry in order to get through the initial stages of the zombie apocalypse in which chaos rules, and how to get through all zombie encounters as the days progress. Finally, you will learn how to adapt to a new world dominated by a zombie plague in order to outlast the epidemic and reshape humanity in a brand new world.

Thanks again for downloading this book, I hope you enjoy it!

Section 1:

The Zombie Apocalypse Begins

A team of students at the University of Leicester used an epidemiological model to determine how many humans would survive a zombie apocalypse. The students in the Department of Physics and Astronomy at the college in the East Midlands of England used the SIR (Susceptible, Infected, and Recovered) model to obtain their conclusions. Scientists have used the SIR model since 1927 to compute the theoretical number of people an infectious outbreak would infect if it spread through a populace, and the Leicester students used the model's equation to determine how a zombie apocalypse would impact humankind.

The SIR model considers the following to determine infection rates:

- The number of susceptible individuals
- The number of infected individuals
- The number of recovered individuals

The outcomes of the research appeared in Leicester's Journal of Special Topics, and the University of Leicester Press Office issued the results on January 5, 2017.

The conclusion made by the students is highly disturbing.

The first set of research results used the following set of criteria to determine the results of a zombie epidemic:

- The population of the world is 7.5 billion people.
- The epidemic began on "day zero" with one zombie.
- The zombies COULD INFECT, but NOT KILL, people who were uninfected.
- Uninfected humans had a 90 percent probability of infection if they encountered a zombie.

- The zombies would die if they did not feed (see note below) within 20 days.

> Note: There are two types of zombies. The first type of zombie is the "beating-heart" zombie, and they must feed to survive, just as a regular human needs food for energy in order to stay alive. The preferred diet of a beating-heart zombie is the brains and intestines of a human, but they will feed upon any part of any living creature, including animals. The second type of zombie is dead and does not have a beating heart or a functioning digestive system. Dead zombies feed upon human flesh, but they do not do it for sustenance; they instinctively feed in order to spread their infection, create more zombies, and keep their species existent. We will discuss this topic in detail later in the book.

The research shows a gradual increase of zombies during the three weeks following the first infection, and then a complete collapse of human existence occurs. The rise of the zombie infection multiplies so rapidly after three weeks that the Leicester research team estimates that there will only be 181 uninfected survivors on the planet on day 100 of the epidemic, and 190 million roaming zombies. When the researchers added three geographic zones into the equation, the spread of the zombie virus was slightly more difficult because the pandemic could not get from zone to zone as easy, but the results are still chilling, as only 273 uninfected humans would be alive in the world on day 100.

Something is missing from the first research study, though, and that is the resourcefulness and resilience of humans to adapt quickly to extreme environments, and fight for their survival. The second study adds those factors into the epidemiological model.

The second set of research results used the following set of criteria to determine the results of a zombie epidemic:

- The population of the world is 7.5 billion people.
- The epidemic began on "day zero" with one zombie.
- The zombies COULD INFECT, but NOT KILL, people who were uninfected.
- Uninfected humans have a 10 percent probability of killing a zombie they encounter.
- Uninfected humans had a 90 percent probability of infection during the initial stage of the zombie epidemic, but the percentage decreased as zombie interfaces increased (In other words, the probability of infection decreased as humans adapted to a zombie's characteristics through experience.)
- The zombies would die if they did not feed within ONE YEAR (as opposed to 20 days in the first study).
- Uninfected human births occurred at the rate of one baby every three years for females capable of conception.

Using the scenario described above in which humans fight and adapt to a zombie infection (see note below), the chances of human survival greatly increase. After 100 days, 200 million humans will be uninfected and involved in a continual struggle to survive, or 2.6 percent of the population from "day zero". After 1,000 days, 67 million humans will remain uninfected by the epidemic, meaning that 99 percent of the earth's population has perished.

Note: There are various types of zombie viruses, and each

variation has unique ways in which it can spread the infection. In some cases, a simple scratch from a zombie can transfer the disease, but in most cases, there must be a cross contamination of blood or saliva between an uninfected human and a zombie in order to pass along the virus. We will discuss this topic in detail later in the book.

After 1,000 days, the uninfected human population begins to rejuvenate, and zombie numbers begin to decline.

Will you be a survivor? Will you have the expertise to overcome the overwhelming obstacles that accompany any infectious disease, especially one that has two feet and an insatiable desire to devour your flesh and transform you into a dreadful beast without a conscience?

If you read this book, you will be provided with the knowledge and skills required to keep your body and soul intact when a zombie infestation occurs, and rest assured, it will one day

How the Zombie Apocalypse Will Occur

Zombies are not your average monster. Zombies were formally human; therefore, they carry some characteristics of their former personhood. However, the character traits that transfer from humanity to zombie-existence are in outward appearance only. Inside the infected beast, there is only chaos as a viscous pathogen takes over the personality of the infected individual. The virus devours the contaminated person's mind and completely releases the essence of their soul from their physical body. A person inflicted by a zombie virus no longer has sympathy or empathy. Their charisma is gone. An empty pit replaces their heart, which could once feel a range of emotions, but now is only a place where involuntary dread lives, leading the empty vessel to feed on flesh in order to obtain a brief moment of relief from a mystifying pain. Although, the desperate emptiness where compassion once made its home never truly subsides until someone executes the zombie.

Viruses that can transform people into zombies do exist, and a pandemic involving one of those contagions is growing more likely every day. The world is getting smaller as the number of human inhabitants soars. Anthropologists believe that the human species dates back to three million years ago, and in 1800, the earth's population saw one billion people for the first time. By 2012, the population had grown to seven billion. Therefore, it took three million years to get to one billion human inhabitants, and from there it took only 212 years for the earth's inhabitants to expand by 6.5 billion more. According to a 2017 report by the United Nations Population Division, the world's human numbers will swell to 10 billion by 2056, which is a 33 percent increase from than the earth's current population of 7.5 billion people. The study shows that human population rates are expanding 1.1 percent each year, which is an average of 80 million people per year.

These population numbers should terrify you.

The expanding population growth presents a challenge to future generations, and to human existence as a whole, because food, water, and fuel resources will grow scarce. The amount of food in the world is not multiplying at the same rate as the human population is expanding, and global starvation is a possibility unless something drastic occurs in technology, or through a corrective measure put into place through a natural process. That "natural process" is the most pressing issue because it will more than likely involve the spread of an infectious disease to reduce dangerously high populations in order for the planet as an entity to survive. As a corrective measure, Mother Nature could introduce a population-clearing virus in a minute anywhere on earth and wipe the planet clean of humankind. Rapidly evolving pathogens have decimated human populations in the past, and natural population control is a common occurrence in the animal kingdom.

Note: In a world with scarce food and clean water supplies, zombies would be in better shape because they do not need either to survive. Essentially, a zombie is a host for a virus, and the only goal of the host virus is to spread, and that is why the zombie is forced by the virus to eat flesh, in order to transfer the disease. Essentially, a virus hacks the hosts genetic instructions, mobilizing it to move even though the body isn't really alive. Since a virus doesn't need food or water to survive because it is not technically a living organism, neither does the zombie body. This gives the zombie an advantage over non-infected humans during an apocalypse because humans not only have to battle zombies to survive, but they also have to search for food and water. We will discuss this topic in detail later in the book.

Pandemics of the Past that Produced Zombie-Like Symptoms

Each century from the past has had its own pandemic in which nature decided to control human population. "Black Death" is the iconic infestation that reduced the earth's human population by an estimated 70 to 200 million people in the 14th Century. The Yersinia pestis bacterium caused the plague, which originated in Central Asia in the late 1330s and eventually spread throughout Europe. The oriental rat flea carried the disease to European ports by way of black rats that were common on merchant ships that traveled Silk Road maritime routes. Once infected, a person would die a horrible death in two to seven days.

In her book *A Distant Mirror: The Calamitous Fourteenth Century*, two-time Pulitzer Prize winning historian Barbara Tuchman described the infected trading ship crews in zombie-like fashion, writing that they arrived "into the harbor of Messina in Sicily with dead and dying men at the oars."

Her description of the men was gruesome, continuing, "The diseased sailors showed strange black swellings about the size of an egg or an apple in the armpits and groin. The swellings oozed blood and pus and were followed by spreading boils and black blotches on the skin from internal bleeding. As the disease spread, other symptoms of continuous fever and spitting of blood appeared instead of the swellings or buboes. In both types everything that issued from the body—breath, sweat, blood from the buboes and lungs, bloody urine and blood-blackened excrement—smelled foul. Depression and despair accompanied the physical symptoms."

At the time, people assumed they were in the midst of an apocalypse—the end of human existence—as the infection spread through rat fleas, direct contact with the bursting external tumors of an infected individual, or through the air. Thirty-three percent of the planet's human population perished in less than a decade as the living dead took victim after victim.

Similar zombie-like epidemics occurred at other times across the world. The horrendous plagues that systematically trimmed the world's population include the following:

- The Plague of Justinian occurred in the Roman Empire between 541 and 542. It is responsible for cutting the population of the world in half as an estimated 100 million people perished. Fleas were responsible for this pandemic as well. Prominent scholar Procopius, who survived the outbreak, wrote in his book *Secret History*, that infected victims were highly delusional and experienced intense nightmares, and experienced swellings and high fevers. Procopius believed Roman Emperor Justinian was the devil or that the gods were punishing him for his many villainous actions.

- In the 16th Century, during the European conquest of Mexico, a smallpox epidemic and two cocoliztli contagions sent fear through the land. The three plagues ravished Mexico, killing 15 million inhabitants and reducing the country's population by 80 percent. The cocolitzli disease spread though the saliva and urine of the vesper mouse or through exposure to the body fluids of an infected individual. The symptoms, as reported by Francisco Hernandez, esteemed royal physician of Phillip II, included severe bleeding from the eyes, nose and mouth, a black tongue, high fever, severe headache and abdominal pain, large nodules behind the ears, and neurological disorders. Death occurred within three to four days after infection.

- The third cholera pandemic from 1852-1860 killed one million people.

- The third plague pandemic from 1894-1903 killed 10 million people.

- The 1918 Spanish Flu ended abruptly in 1919 after it had afflicted one-third of the world's population. As many as 50 million people died with approximately 25 million of those deaths occurring in the first 25 weeks of the outbreak. Medical researchers believe that the virus originated with birds before it swiftly mutated and attacked humans. Physicians said the pandemic's victims developed dark spots on their cheeks and turned blue as their lungs filled with a frothy, bloody substance that suffocated them.

- The 1968-1969 Hong Kong flu killed one million people.

- The 1957-1958 Asian flu killed two million people.

- The 1989-1990 flu pandemic killed one million people.

- As of 2015, 35 million people have died from HIV/AIDS virus-related illnesses. The disease originated in West Africa through human contact with the blood of infected chimpanzees.

Note: The American colony of Roanoke was established by England in 1587. In all, 115 men and women became a part of the first permanent English settlement in the "new world". The colonists built sound and secure structures and had enough food and supplies to last them a significant amount of time. In 1590, a supply ship returned to find that all of the colonists were gone. Harvard archeologist Lawrence Stager found evidence of cannibalism at the site where they were left, and reports from the local base of Native Americans said that the colonists themselves were the result of their vanishing. It is believe that an undead virus spread through the colony, and the zombie-infected settlers feasted upon one another until they were no more.

Zombies experience many of the symptoms and conditions of those infected by the plagues of the past, including oozing pus or blood, rotting flesh and buboes, a ferocious smell, extreme pain, vomiting of blood, blank stares, moaning, body convulsions, lack of bladder control, and neurological and psychological disruption. The neurological and psychological disorder associated with people infected by a virus causes madness, which is certainly a zombie characteristic as the nervous system succumbs to an out-of-mind experience, reducing a person to something that is no longer human.

Public health officials worry about the next pandemic because a massive population-reducing virus is imaginable. While there is plenty of space on the planet for humans to occupy, most individuals choose to live in metropolitan areas with dense populations, and that concentration of people is extremely disconcerting if a zombie virus incubates inside one of them. The other concern is the ability for people to travel easily and quickly by numerous means of transportation, which could cause a pathogen to spread across multiple contents in a blaze. In addition, researchers are discovering new infectious diseases on a daily basis, and many of these viruses have the ability to mutate rapidly. The spread of a zombie pathogen would be fast and escape nearly impossible, especially for those who are unprepared. Numerous viruses exist that could modify into a pathogen that could create zombies.

Note: The most dangerous places to live on day zero of a zombie apocalypse are areas with the highest populations coupled with highest density of people per square kilometer because the zombie virus will travel fast, and there are limited options for leaving the area quickly. The most susceptible major regions are East Asia (Japan, China, South Korea, and Taiwan), South Asia (India, Pakistan, Bangladesh, Sri Lanka, Nepal, and

Maldives), Northwest Europe (UK, Germany, France, Netherlands, Poland, Ireland, Denmark, Spain, Portugal, Italy, Belgium, and Luxembourg), and Eastern North America (Northeast United States and Southeast Canada). Other trouble areas include the Nile Valley in Egypt, the coastal areas of Nigeria, Central Mexico, and the coastal areas of Venezuela, Peru, Brazil, and Argentina. We will discuss this topic in detail later in the book.

Natural Regulation of Populations in the Animal Kingdom

Wild animals often control their own populations, which is something that modern humans, who rely on consciousness more than instinct, are not prone to do. Rudy Boonstra, a professor of zoology in the Division of Life Sciences at the University of Toronto at Scarborough, studied this phenomenon.

"No population of organisms increases without limit," Boonstra tells Science Daily. "The central question in population ecology is what regulates their numbers. And the answer is this: the actions of the populations themselves. The populations themselves are critical to preventing unlimited growth."

Along with researcher Tim Karels, Boonstra studied the arctic ground squirrel to determine what they would do if presented with varying population challenges, which for the squirrel involves food availability and exposure to predators.

"Animals can change their reproductive output depending on certain environmental conditions. And one of those environmental conditions is population density," Karels says. "So if you have lots of neighbors and you're competing for the same food, it can lower reproduction.

At very high population densities, female ground squirrels basically shut down their reproduction, and that was done in order to sustain their own survival. When conditions were better, they would start reproducing again."

This type of population control is common in the animal kingdom. These measures assure the survival of the species through self-regulation that is instinctive. Even natural wildfires are self-regulators that play a role in maintaining ecosystems. Certain flora relies on canopy fires to provide conditions that are ripe for germination. Trees in the forest have adapted over time to produce seeds only after a fire has occurred, and the forest's population of deer, elk and other fauna, thrive on the vegetation that springs up across burned woodland floors.

However, humans do not self-regulate their populations and often congregate into high-density populaces, which place them in danger of an outside force controlling their outcomes, and that usually occurs through a pathogen that indiscriminately kills large groups of people. These infectious diseases run rampant to protect all life on earth, so that resources don't run so scarce that *all* flora and fauna disappear. Nature guarantees that a great human plague is on the horizon, and it is very likely that that fast-approaching pandemic will come in the form of a zombie apocalypse.

Zombie Prophecy

There is also prophecy regarding zombies. Hailed prophet Nostradamus, who studied astrology and the occult, writes in *The Prophecies*, "Not far from the age of the millennium, when there is no more room in Hell, the buried dead shall come out of their graves. The 16th

Century seer predicted the French Revolution, Hitler and World War II, the Great London Fire, the moon landing, the 9/11 terrorist attacks, and many other incidents, so his zombie apocalypse prediction should be taken seriously.

In addition, the Quran states that the apocalypse will commence when wild tribes "swiftly swarm from every mound" and devour everything in sight. Also, the Bible references an impending zombie apocalypse, forecasting a plague that will strike down evil forces, saying, "Their flesh will rot while they are standing on their feet, their eyes will rot in their sockets, and their tongues will rot in their mouths." The Bible does not refer to the death of these infected beings; it describes the victims of wrath as walking corpses.

Note: European tales speak of "revenants" climbing out of their graves to spread disease. One story that took place near Burton upon Trent in East Staffordshire, England, says that two revenants—corpses returning from the dead—woke up each evening, walked into the town, and spoke to passing villagers, who would proceed to get sick and die the following day. To permanently dispose of the walking corpses, the villagers waited for the two zombies to return to their graves, dug them up, and cut off their heads and ripped out their hearts. The revenants were never seen again.

Current Zombie Pathogens and Pathogenic Fungus

It is unclear which pathogen or neurotoxin will lead to a zombie apocalypse, but there are already the conditions in place for one to occur. Many of the planet's current collection of pathogens are ripe for an explosion of apocalyptic proportions, especially when you consider that the earth's diseases and toxins will adapt and mutate as the years progress and the number of potential hosts multiplies extravagantly as the population of the world explodes.

In addition, experiments with neurotoxins, zombie-like viruses, and stem cells could lead us down a disastrous path to total human annihilation. The most prominent case of those things commingling inside of a lab has already occurred within the last year, leading to disastrous consequences in a town northwest of Mexico City, if the reports are true. At the end of this section, the case will be examined, uncovering perplexing and utterly grim results that could be a signal that the zombie apocalypse has already begun. However, before we get there, let's examine the many ways an unsuspecting mind can be controlled, creating a zombie, in modern times.

Mind-controlling Fungus, Parasites, and Viruses

In 2011, reports circled that million of flies had turned to zombies in Washington, D.C. A mind-controlling fungus attacked the flies and manipulated their behavior. Essentially, the fungus was attempting to control the over-population of flies, in a natural way, by causing them to move to a high point and freeze, which allowed the wind to carry the fungus's spores into the air to attack other flies.

Mike Raupp, a University of Maryland entomologist, told NPR that the fungus "zombie-izes" the insects, saying, "We were getting literally hundreds of reports of these crazy, dead flies everywhere—on vegetation, on sign posts."

No one complains too much when it comes to the mass extermination of the common fly, which provides little more than an irritant to people, but a zombie infection began attacking honeybees in 2012, and a different type of fly was the carrier of the disease. The tiny, parasitoid phorid fly called *Apocephalus borealis* lands on the bee, lays eggs in its abdomen, and several days later, the bee bumbles to its death.

The bee's final flight begins without warning, as it heads out of its hive, looking for light, before spinning out of control. After the bee's death, the phorid fly larvae burrow out from the bee's neck to begin the process anew. Andrew Core, a lead researcher of a published study on the phenomenon, said the bees were acting "like a zombie."

"When we observed the bees for some time—the ones that were alive—we found that they walked in circles, often with no sense of direction," Core said in a statement from San Francisco State University.

Parasites that control the minds of the living organism they infect are common. They steal nutrients from their hosts while offering nothing in return, systematically destroying the infected life form's neurotransmitters or hormones. There are so many types of parasites currently in existence that many are a mystery to researchers. Janice Moore, author of *Parasites and the Behavior of Animals* and a professor at Colorado State University, told NPR, "If you take the world of parasites broadly, we don't know the half of it yet."

Toxoplasma Gondii, the Zombie Cat Parasite

When a rat is infected by *Toxoplasma Gondii*, it changes the brain chemistry of the rodent. Normally, a rat avoids the scent of its natural predator, the cat, thereby escaping a deadly attack, but *Toxoplasma* infection causes the rat to be drawn to the smell of felines and their urine, making it a zombie and disarming the rodent's defense mode. Once the rat is hooked to the cat through a new set of desires that are overtly abnormal, and sexual in nature, the feline devours the rat, and the cat becomes infected itself. That parasite can then be transferred to humans through cat's feces or feces-infected water. In addition, the virus lives within many farm animals, so it can make its way into the bodies of a human host through undercooked meat.

Since the beginning of the 20th Century, when domestic cat ownership began to become popular, the percentage of people with schizophrenia began to increase. Many medical researchers believe that schizophrenia, a disorder that affects a person's ability to connect with reality, could be linked to *Toxoplasma Gondii*.

Note: A schizophrenic disorder known as Cotard delusion, or walking corpse syndrome, causes victims to think they have died, that their soul is missing, and their flesh is rotting. The disorder was first reported by Jules Cotard, a French neurologist, in 1880. It is possible that a parasite or virus caused the victims of Cotard delusion to detach from real life.

It is estimated that 30 percent of the people living on the planet, or about two billion individuals, are carrying the parasite in their brains. Research also shows that the parasite can be passed from parents to their children, and it can lead to death or severe brain damage to the fetus's of infected women.

Once infected with the parasite, the protozoan lives inside the brain cells of its host, lying dormant, or so it has been thought by experts for many years. However, there is a growing collection of evidence that reveals a different outcome, including a study by Czech evolutionary biologist Jaroslav Flegr, who works at

Charles University in Prague. His study showed that male subjects who tested positive for *Toxoplasma* had delayed reaction times and were generally less attentive.

Bob Yolken, chairperson of Pediatric Neurovirology at John Hopkins medical school told NPR, "Studies have looked at accidents—individuals in automobile accidents, both drivers and pedestrians—and they have increased rates of *Toxoplasma*."

In the Flegr study, the infected men were also more suspicious and introverted, which are common characteristics of schizophrenics. In addition, they were unmindful and disagreeable to rules, withdrawn, antisocial, and hostile. Infected women, though not impacted like the males, were more attracted to the men, who showed increased levels of testosterone when afflicted with the parasite.

Since 30 percent of the world's population is estimated to be infected by the parasite, researchers believe that it is affecting the patterns of behavior in large geographic areas or large populations of people where it is more prevalent, and that as it mutates, could become more controlling and easier to spread.

"I believe it can have this impact," Flegr told *Vice*. "It was already published by another parasitologist that national personality can be partially explained by frequency of toxoplasmosis."

Soon this "smart" parasite or another like it could mutate to the point where it controls entire countries, making its inhabitants mindless, disagreeable, fearless, and hostile zombies, which could lead to aggressive posturing, a world war, and the end of humankind. This could be already be playing out within the more rancorous regions of the world.

Rabies, Bullet-Shaped Brain Manipulators

Dr. Jonathon Dinman, an esteemed researcher and professor in the Department of Cell Biology and Molecular Genetics at the University of Maryland, has a story to tell, and it is about zombies. He is on record as saying that he believes that the zombie virus already exists, and it is rabies.

The viral disease, which is contracted through salivary transmission from the bite of an infected host, is bullet-shaped and often escapes detection by the body's immune system. The disease takes over the host's cells and creates copies of itself. As its numbers grow, the virus moves to the brain, seeking out specific neurotransmitters in an effort to increase the bodies response to fear, which heightens aggression. The victim also becomes more sensitive, in a painful way, to outside stimuli, causing them to twitch, and become defensive and unpredictable, as the mouth foams with frothy, infected saliva.

"Infection is nearly 100 percent lethal; it turns you into the walking dead, and causes you to change your behavior by reprogramming you to bite other people to spread the infection," Dinman told *Red Orbit*. "Now, if only it kept the corpse walking around."

Dinman had a response to that idea as well. Rabies is known to keep the host's body alive for only a few days in a mind-controlled state, but the possibility of a longer death sentence is not out of the question.

"So, you start with the rabies virus, but you engineer it so that it doesn't actually kill you. It just takes over you brain and makes you want to bite other people to spread itself. Infected people just become automators devoted to spreading the virus. The main viral property you'd want to change would be to convert it from causing an acute infection, like Ebola, which tends to kill the victim quickly, to a persistent infection like herpes, which stays with you for your entire life. Functions you'd want the infected person to retain would be metabolism, so they can produce more virus, and motility, so they can get from victim to victim."

Virus mutations naturally occur through copying mistakes during gene replication, damage from ultraviolet light, or the swapping of genetic code with other viruses, which is called "reassortment" or "recombination", according to Elankumaran Subbiah. Take rabies, Dinman's factors, along with the ability to spread quickly through the air like that of the flu virus, and a scenario is in place that could dismantle humanity by way of zombies.

> Note: A zombie apocalypse requires a virus that causes the immediate death and reanimation of its host. Most of today's strains of viruses require a prolonged incubation of a week or more before symptoms surface and death occurs. However, the genetic codes of many viruses are changing in dramatic ways on a daily basis to bypass the host's immune system, creating shorter incubation times. We will discuss this topic in detail later in the book.

Other Mind-Altering Viruses and Parasites

There are numerous other potential dangers in the world that cause a bizarre change in the characteristics of the host body. When discussing the potential dangers in the world that could lead to a zombie apocalypse, Joanne Webster, a parasitologist at London's Imperial College, said, "The brain is a privileged site for many parasites. And that really challenges the concept of free will—after all, is it 'us' our parasites who decide our behavior?"

It is a great question, and certainly the bottom line notion when it comes to the future of humanity. What viral or parasitic mutation will eventually control us, and how? For, it is sure to happen, as we orientate ourselves in that direction with every day.

Research has also shown that when two viruses fight for control of the same host, increasing erratic behavior occurs. Considering that there are at least 32,000 viruses that can infect mammals, according to a report in a journal published by the American Society for Microbiology, the possibilities of multiple viruses infecting one individual and creating chaotic outcomes is always possible. The following are examples of current zombie-inducing viruses and parasites.

- *Naegleria fowleri* is found in warm stagnant waters. Once inside the human body, it has an appetite for human brain tissue. The process begins as a cyst, but once it makes contact with a host, it grows tentacles called pseudopods and turns into a trophozoite. The trophozoite follows nerve fibers in order to find the central nervous system. Once it finds the brain, it burrows into the tissue, devouring cells. The human it infects notices changes in tastes and smells, grows a fever and begins to stiffen. Confusion follows, focus is lost, and hallucinations begin. A Taiwanese man survived 25 days with the amoeba devouring his brain after he contracted it from a hot spring's resort, but most victims last only last a few weeks.

- "African sleeping sickness" is a disease caused by *Trypososoma*, a parasite that is carried by the tsetse fly. The tsetse fly has a thirst for human blood, and the parasite is transferred to a human host through a fly's bite. During a slow painful process, the parasite enters its victim and alters its brain cells. The parasites are particularly attracted to the hypothalamus, a regulator of mood and sleep cycles. The parasitic flagellate protozoa makes melatonin levels in the body malfunction causing headaches and an alteration of sleep patterns. Depression, loss of appetite, itching, tremors, and unintelligible speech patterns develop over a few years, until the infected individual eventually becomes unresponsiveness and lethargic, which finally leads to prolonged instances of sleep, coma, and death.

- The influenza virus is adapting in immeasurable degrees, mutating through every season and becoming stronger with every passing year. With that evolving strength, its capability to alter minds progresses as well. Research has found that the virus is making people more sociable. Before flu symptoms occur, humans are drawn to people, especially large groups of people. Studies reveal that flu victims are more likely than healthy individuals to go to populated places like bars and house parties. Considering that the 1918 Spanish Flu killed 50 million, this is a very dangerous mutation that could advance even further and cause an apocalypse.

- A zombie fungus called *Ophiocordyceps unilateralis* causes ants in Thailand, Africa, and Brazil to pull of their usual course and die. Ants called *Camponotus leonardi* are infected by the entomopathogen on the forest floor when one of the fungus's spores lands on it. The insect-pathogenising fungus develops for several days inside the ant's body, and when the fungal parasite is ready to complete its life cycle, it forces the ant into a zombie state. The insect blindly climbs a tree to a spot with suitable humidity for the fungus to grow. Then, the ant bites down on a leave to anchor itself and dies. Within 24 hours, a stalk grows out of the ant's head and unleashes spores across the forest floor below.

- A hairworm, a parasitoid animal, begins its lifecycle inside the larva of an insect such as a mosquito. The insect larva, containing the parasite, is then eaten by a cricket. Next, the hairworm begins to reach maturity inside the cricket, but to continue its lifecycle, the hairworm needs to be near a body of water. Since crickets do not intentionally go near water or attempt to swim in it, the hairworm alters the function of the cricket's central nervous system, driving it into the closest water source. The cricket drowns, and the worms, sometimes as many as two dozen, emerge from within the cricket and reproduce.

- The emerald cockroach wasp is a metallic-colored insect that glows with emeralds and reds, and is known to destroy its hosts. Found in the tropics of Africa, Asia, and the Pacific islands, the insect paralyzes roaches with a single sting, and then takes over its mind. A serum of neurotransmitters is emitted into the roach's brain, turning it into a zombie. After chewing off the roach's antenna, the wasp rides the roach to its lair. Once the mindless roach arrives, the wasp lays eggs on its abdomen. During the entire process, the roach is alive, but remains submissive even as the wasp larva eat it alive.

Note: In the National Geographic documentary *The Truth Behind Zombies*, Samita Andreansky, a virologist at the University of Miami, said, "Sure, I could imagine a scenario where you mix rabies with a flu virus to get airborne transmission, a measles virus to get personality changes, the encephalitis virus to cook your brain with fever, and throw in the Ebola virus to cause you to bleed from your guts. Combine all these things, and you'll get something like the zombie virus."

Sorcerers and Haitian Zombie Neurotoxins

Many Haitians believe in zombies, and they also believe that sorcery is the cause of a human's zombie state. Local Haitian lore suggests that bokors (sorcerers) capture a person's soul, creating an existing shell that functions in physicality alone. Essentially, they become the walking dead. During these ceremonies to capture a spirit and create a living corpse, the bokor gives the victim a complex mix of powders from plants and animals.

Dr. Nathan S. Kline, who was a researcher in the field of psychology before his death, studied eight samples of Haitian ritualistic powders used by bokors during zombie-transition ceremonies. All of the samples had varying ingredients but four components were in each of the eight samples, which included human remains, as well as the remnants from poisonous hyla tree frogs, toxic marine toads, and puffer fish, which contain a neurotoxin that is deadly to humans.

Kline's research proved that the toxic concoction—not the rituals themselves—created zombies, people with walking paralysis. The victim's skin would become irritated and raw and their self-awareness would disappear. In some cases, the inflicted person's heart would slow to a nearly lifeless pace, and the person would appear to be dead. Often, these people in a zombie state would be laid to rest, only to awaken before or after burial.

Numerous documented tales exist regarding the death and resurrection of Haitians. In some cases, the poisoned people would be fed an alkaloid, an organic nitrogen-containing drug, which brought them back to existence, but not entirely; they would have amnesia and remain in a trance-like state for their remaining days on earth, only able to perform basic functions. Many Haitians believe that these zombies have been sold into slavery and placed on sugar plantations to work without resistance for the rest of their lives.

Necro-Mortosis Zombies

In 2006, amid a controversial Haitian presidential election, something odd occurred in Cité Soleil, a densely populated and impoverished slum on the outskirts of Port-au-Prince, Haiti: a bewildering virus came to life. The initial reports were that the Necro-Mortosis infection was only a curse, or even a hoax perpetrated by the losers of the election in Haiti to create fear and chaos among Haitian citizens to make the new regime's job more difficult.

The virus was no hoax, and it certainly wasn't a curse.

Reports concerning the virus said that it "reanimated" or "zombified" its victims, even though it began innocently enough, with flu-like symptoms, consisting of aching muscles, headache, chills, and fever. However, as the infection progressed, it slowed the victim's heart, created lethargy, and caused disorientation. Within 48 hours, necrosis, or the death of the body's cells, occurred, and after the cells ceased to operate and the victim was dead by all clinical definitions, reanimation proceeded within minutes.

The pathogen wasn't taken seriously until it leapt out of the Haitian ghetto of Cité Soleil and into mainstream society. Since the victims of the virus are not subject to immediate death and instantaneous reanimation, and the initial symptoms of the virus are minor and resemble those of the flu, unknowing victims of the infection spread the disease quickly. The contagion crossed the Haitian border to the Dominican Republic in less than a month after the first infection, followed by a few cases that popped up in Puerto Rico, presumably spread by an air traveler as the virus crossed the Caribbean Sea from Santa Domingo to San Juan, a 254-mile trek.

The virus transfers from the host to non-infected individuals through the exchange of body fluids such as saliva, blood, or semen. It is not airborne, and therefore, can only spread through a bite, an infected syringe, or sex. By the end of 2006, medical professionals reported cases in South America, Central America, Southern Europe, Eastern Europe, the Middle East, and parts of Asia.

UCLA Professor David Whister published a paper in the *Scientific Journal of Medicine* in 2007 that explained the odd phenomenon.

"All viruses consist of a package of genetic material surrounded by a protein and lipid shell. The type A Necro-Mortosis virus consists of seven proteins and eight strands of ribonucleic acid (RNA), which carry the code for making the proteins."

The concern with the Necro-Mortis virus is found in the etymology of its name. "Necro" is a Greek prefix meaning "death" or "dead tissue", or is relative to a corpse. "Mortis" is much of the same in definition, for it is Latin for "death". The word "mortis" is often coupled with "rigor" to create "rigor mortis", which is used to identify the third stage of death in which the corpse becomes stiff, but "rigor" isn't needed to identify Necro-Mortis, and Whister explains why.

"The key that lead us here was the fact that rigor mortis did not set in," he said. "We knew this must be significant to the whole process. Now we understand that the virus 'allows' the body this last motor function in order to be able to seek nutritional sustenance for the virus in a form that can only be found in warm blood and flesh."

Since then, the virus has been kept mostly under wraps by governments around the world, and the CDC (Center for Disease Control and Prevention), a United States federal agency, denies the existence of the virus even as virologists are simultaneously studying the virus and reporting the results to the general public. In addition, medical facilities are documenting cases, and national public health and safety organizations are regulating interaction with those who are infected.

In 2012, CDC spokesperson David Daigle told the *HuffPost*, the "CDC does not know of a virus or condition that would reanimate the dead, or one that would present zombie-like symptoms."

Along with Whister's reporting, a Necro-Mortosis study was conducted by the British Caduceus Society to find out if the virus inflicted particular types of people based on genetic factors such as race. The lead researchers, Dr. Stephen H. Dixel and professor Paul James Buxton, performed a six-month study of numerous documented cases in Europe, and their research revealed that men are three times more likely to become infected by the virus.

"I am not suggesting that men are more vulnerable to the virus." Dixel said, "In fact anyone who introduces the virus into their bodies blood stream will no doubt develop full blown Mortosis usually within 48 hours. What I am saying is that men seem to be more prone to exposure. They take greater risks. Fight or flight, defend their territory. This often leads to unpleasant results."

The virus does not discriminate; it will annihilate anyone it drops upon; however, it just appears that women are more intelligent and avoid exposure to the virus.

"Women often reduce the risk of infection by simply avoiding the possibility of exposure. They rarely go seeking confrontation with an undead. Whereas many times men are in a situation that does bring on a physical interaction with a Mortosis sufferer. Most front line undead defense teams, police and soldiers are male. Most zombie hunters are also male. This dynamic is changing slowly but for the most part it stands."

The good news is that in 2007, Amcalon Corporation, a pharmaceutical company, began testing a drug called

XL-6, which has shown some ability to slow the symptoms of the Mortosis infection.

"The tests are still in their preliminary stages," an Amcalon spokesperson said in a released statement. "We need to duplicate the effect in many ways before moving forward with development of a possible vaccine."

The not-so-good news is that the paper also stated that a human subject that contracted the virus was given the inhibitor with promising initial results that came with a devastating conclusion.

"Typically an exposed person will begin showing signs of decay and mortification within one or two days," the spokesperson This subject was able to offset the effects of Necro-Mortosis for seven days. During which time he was in a healthy and stable condition."

On the seventh day, the subject developed severe flu symptoms, the central nervous system was attacked, and reanimation occurred. The victim was euthanized on the eight day. The Amcalon Corporation continued trial studies and better results followed.

In 2014, the first incident of Necro-Mortis occurred in the United States. A woman went into labor in Portland, Washington, and tests revealed that she had contracted the zombie virus. Since she was in the early stages of infection, she was restrained and monitored closely, but allowed to give birth. Once the child was born, the woman's life was terminated, and the baby was found to have trace amounts of the virus in its system.

According to Dr. Linda Pharsooc, a virologist with Johns Hopkins Children's Center, who worked on the case, the infant who was born at Miller Children's Hospital was given phase four XL-6, and within a week, the baby had no traces of Necro-Mortosis in her system. After five weeks, the baby, which was named Miracle, was still alive, healthy, and without the virus.

"This has to be done in a clinical trial setting, because really the only way we can prove that we've accomplished remission in this case is by taking the child off treatment, and that's not without risks," Pharsooc released in a statement. "At this time, there is no plan to stop treatment."

The treatment continued for a year, and then the child mysteriously disappeared. It was reported by Pharsooc after the disappearance that the baby was placed in a foster home in order to protect its anonymity, as it continued to receive XL-6 treatments. Although, even Pharsooc was a skeptic at the time of the initial reporting, confirming that she do not see the fostering take place, and claiming that that the possibility exists that the child could have died or was taken to a laboratory for observation and study. Soon afterwards, Pharsooc distanced from the story, and now, no longer practices medicine and refuses all interviews.

As cases of Necro-Mortosis continue to surface, Amcalon has not released any new information regarding ongoing research sine April 29, 2014. In a press release, they reported that they were joining forces with UK based company Forward Thrust to further develop a synthetic blood substitute, and would release results of their testing in "late 2016-early 2017". No information has been reported as of yet, and we were unable to reach anyone from Amcalon for comment.

The Reanimation of the Mummies of Guanajuato, Mexico

Before his disappearance, Claude Martin Begnaud, a professor in the department of Biochemistry at Cambridge University, ran a covert program funded by Britain's Royal Centre for Defence Medicine, which investigated the possibility of reanimating the dead. In 2013, Begnaud's team transferred a mutated virus that had the ability to resurrect dead cells into donated medical research corpuses. Essentially, the virus infected the exterminated cells of the corpse, and used the cell's remaining organelles to bring it back to life in order to clone the virus's DNA.

According to documents obtained by *The Daily Telegraph* from an anonymous source who was a research assistant at the time, the corpses reanimated into human life forms as their mutated cells began to rejuvenate, after a five to seven day viral incubation period. The documents explain that the corpses "retained many of the characteristics of their former human self."

After several successful experiments, Cambridge University shut down the program because the corpuses began acting erratically. The lead researchers described the reanimated corpses' behavior as "harmful and aggressive psychosis" with an "intolerance to communication, and an inability to show any positive social behavior," punctuated with the caveat, "we felt we were in danger whenever we were studying them closely."

While Begnaud wished to continue the study, even as he admitted that the animated corpses were growing more dangerous as the days proceeded, the university wanted no part of it. The research group exterminated each of the zombies by using a captive bolt pistol, which drives a penetrating metal bar through the brain of its victims, and is normally reserved for euthanizing animals like cows before they are slaughtered. The project seemed to be a tale of caution and a sensible retreat in the end; however, Begnaud, who believed his research could lead to longer life spans, left the university to explore the experiment's possibilities elsewhere.

In November 2016, Begnaud and two other members of his research group resurfaced in Guanajuato, Mexico. Guanajuato is known for two things: its network of defunct mining tunnels under the city and its collection of mummies.

In the early 1860s, hundred of corpses were interred in crypts in Guanajuato after a cholera epidemic. In a rare occurrence, many of the corpses inside the above ground crypt were naturally mummified through a combination of heat and low humidity inside the tomb's cement walls. The deceased's hair and clothes were still intact when they were extracted many years later and put on display at the Museo de Las Momias de Guanajuato. Today, visitors will find all manner of mummies from infants to a pregnant woman and everything in between. Out of the 111 mummies that were removed, museum visitors can inspect 59 that are on permanent display. Each of the corpse's faces is alive with an eternal expression of horror at their final fate, as their soul left their body.

Author Ray Bradbury once visited the catacombs at Guanajuato, and in the introduction of his short story "The Next in Line", he wrote, "The experience so wounded and terrified me, I could hardly wait to flee Mexico. I had nightmares about dying and having to remain in the halls of the dead with those propped and wired bodies."

The remaining mummies, which were storied in a closed catacomb below the city went missing in March 2017, and it is reported that Begnaud purchased the bodies, took them to a lab within the city, and began practicing the research he had left behind in Cambridge. The process he used in England to reanimate corpses worked again with great success, but with a more horrifying twist.

The first three mummified bodies that were injected with Begnaud's serum and left overnight, were nowhere to be found the following morning. After searching the lab facility and its grounds, the bewildered scientists believed that someone must have entered the facility and tampered with their subjects. After a few days of investigation into the disappearance with no results, Begnaud redid the experiment and then sat back and watched the progress of his research unfold before him. After five hours, the mummies reanimated, and the excited team rushed into the lab to document the results, but they were met with tragedy.

Just recently, Miguel Andre, a member of the team, and the proclaimed only survivor of the group, came forward to discuss the experiment with the newspaper *La Cronica de Baja California*. The serum they used, named 29ID-HHQ, mixed the mutated, cell-invigorating virus along with fetal stem cells that rejuvenate deteriorating flesh, bone, and muscle, as well as extracts from the psychoactive plants ayahuasca and jimsonweed, which block all instances of adenosine receptor rejuvenation in humans, while stimulating neurotransmitters such as dopamine, acetylcholine, serotonin, and norepinephrine. Also included within the injection was a small amount of tetrodotoxin from a toadfish.

"We knew the virus reanimated living cells, but we felt we needed to advance the serum," Andre, an evolutionary virologist from Lisbon, said. "Basically, we were trying to figure out a way to stimulate dead neurotransmitters into firing again. In the end, we essentially created Frankenstein's monster. Actually, it was much worse, and we couldn't control the outcome. The mummy took on the characteristics of a zombie, including an insatiable appetite for human flesh, and make no mistake about it, these were beasts with zero empathy."

The first victim was Dr. Byron Johnson, who worked as a virology consultant at the Queen Elizabeth Hospital Birmingham, before he was assigned to the Royal Centre for Defence Medicine during the Cambridge experiments. He left with Begnaud and Andre to continue their research.

"In an instant, half of Dr. Johnson's face was eaten and he crumbled to the ground," the scholar from Portugal said, "but moments later, he awoke and came after me and Claude, along with his three attackers, in a formidable rage. It just wasn't Byron anymore. He wasn't human."

According to Andre, he escaped the lab as Begnaud was being devoured. Cambridge University and the municipality of Guanajuato have denied all claims of involvement. However, in the past three months, dozens of disappearances have been reported in the town's newspaper *Correo de Guanajuato*, describing "feral humans" who "hiss and gnash their teeth", and sometimes chase pedestrians through the 19th century silver mining tunnels below the colonial city. The mining tunnels are no longer operational after the city's occupants extracted all of the silver years ago, but a subterranean labyrinth exists, and part of it is used as network of roads for the community's citizens. Apparently, the underground maze has become home for a new form of human life.

"There is no more esteemed serial killer than the mother of our earth," Andre said in *La Cronica*. "Creative and beguiling, she moves to initiate life, while simultaneously destroying those things that become too powerful and too selfish to adequately share space and be a good neighbor to other living organisms. Humanity will be her next victim, and I am sorry to say that our research team quite possibly spawned the apocalypse. If the virus spreads to a large city like Mexico City, which is 200 miles southeast of Guanajuato, it will be the end of humanity."

A potential government cover-up is occurring, and it could be detrimental to human survival, according to Andre. It is safe to say that the strong will survive any virus that is currently real or yet to be imagined through intelligence, cleverness, physicality, and pure will. The rest of this book is designed to provide you with the mental and physical skills to beat the altered soul of the planet when zombies come to march upon our terrain.

Note: Miguel Andre is a credible virologist, who received a Lasker Award of Special Achievement in 2012 for numerous fundamental discoveries concerning the nature of genes.

Section 2:

Zombie Characteristics and Abilities

Before we can defeat zombies and survive an apocalypse, we must first understand how a zombie operates. There lies the problem. There is uncertainty in regards to what type of zombie we might face as the world falls apart, so we must know and understand every possibility of predator that we fight face. However, we do know that most modern zombie experts give them five key characteristics:

- <u>A zombie has been reanimated back to life in one way or another</u>. It could be that the zombie was actually dead, or the other possibility is that the rotting beast could have been in a coma-like state and only appeared as if it had left our mortal plane. Regardless, a zombie is "alive" because its brain is functioning in some form or fashion. If the zombie was once dead, it only becomes alive through the reinvigoration of its brain cells into functioning again, even while the rest of its body continues to decay until there is nothing left of it.

- <u>A contagion has infected a zombie, which has led to its reanimation</u>. The infection could by a parasite, a virus, a fungus, radiation, or something that is not completely understood by humanity in scientific terms, such as a curse placed upon the planet by an angry god. Normally, the contagion is passed to a non-infected individual through the transfer of body fluids. Sometimes, the transfer can take place through something as simple as contact with the zombie, while other types of zombies can transmit their contagion through a bite or a scratch.

- <u>A zombie is aggressive in order to spread the disease it carries</u>. It is acting on instinct, like a parasite. In order for the disease to survive, it needs to spread, and that can only be done through some aggressive means. A zombie becomes a predator, and you become its prey.

- <u>A Zombie does not fully understand the environment in which it wreaks havoc</u>. It does not appreciate that it was once a functioning human that has transitioned into a monster. Basically, a zombie is a soulless creature with no empathy and no understanding of reality.

- <u>Zombies reach a permanent end when their brain isn't charging anymore</u>. Once a Zombie's brain has been destroyed through some sort of weaponry, it ceases to function as an enemy combatant. There are ways to immobilize a zombie, and the body deteriorates and die as it progresses to the end stage of decay, so destroying the brain isn't the only way to stop a zombie in its tracks. A zombie can be injured, and as you will see in the zombie decay section of the book, it will cease to function on a physical level in time as its body rots away.

Beyond those five things, the varieties of zombie are limitless, and even those five things are not a constant in some variations of zombie. Therefore, a full list of possibilities is required in order to survive the day the dreadful apocalypse comes when we are fighting to save ourselves as well as the entirety of the human race.

Note: A jiangshi, meaning "stiff corpse", and also called a "Chinese Hopping Zombie", is a living dead creature described by Qing Dynasty scholar Ji Xiaolan in his book *Yuewei Caotang Biji*. Because of rigor mortis, the hopping zombie hops as its main means of mobility with its arms extended in front of it for balance. The legend says that the zombie is resurrected through a supernatural act in order to seek out the life force of the living and gain enough strength to become fully human again. Its victims become hopping zombies themselves, and the loop continues endlessly.

Stages of Zombie Decay

Zombies do decompose. While their brains have been reanimated to life, giving the zombie a new sense of purpose, the rest of their body is carried along for the ride in a rotting state of decay. Infections do not break from the laws of nature, even it is a zombie virus. While every virus has its peculiarities and various mutations, most of them follow a particular pattern of incubation and attack, and we shouldn't assume that a zombie virus would be any different. Infections spark certain parts of the body to life, but they are also responsible for the decay of their unused portions. There are five stages of zombie decay.

- Stage 1: Blue Crispy. The first stage of zombie decay occurs when the heart stops pumping blood through the body. The lack of oxygen creates a bluish hue to the skin and the corpse's muscles tighten, causing stiffness. Also, the structural integrity of the body's cells begin to crumble, which releases enzymes into the body. Enzymes are a terror to dead human tissue because they accelerate chemical reactions and immediately begin to break it down. Sometimes, this causes blisters to form on the body. These fresh blue and blistery zombies are called "blue crispies".

- Stage 2: Bloater. After 24 hours, the zombie's body begins to bloat as internal gases begin to build up. This process pushes body fluids out of every orifice. The digestive track pushes out waste and acid from the anus, penis, and vagina, depending on the zombie's equipment. The nose, mouth, and ears ooze blood, pus, and mucous. Because of the leaking liquids, the zombie is most contagious when it is a bloater.

- Stage 3: Dripper. Before zombies proceed to becoming mostly bone, they begin to dissolve through a state of putrefaction. This stage of decay progresses slowly as flesh appears to be melting of the zombie's frame. As with any dead flesh, microorganisms consume and slowly dissolve it. The zombie's skin becomes toxic, turning a blackish-green, as putrefied liquid falls from the bone. The higher the humidity and temperature, the faster the zombie dissolves. Cold temperatures will be kinder to the zombie and its deteriorating flesh. Nests of insect larvae may be visible on portions of a dripper's flesh, and the stench is considerable as it would be with any decomposing matter.

- <u>Stage 4: Boner</u>. In this state, the zombie's flesh has rotted off, and bones and tendons are all that is visible. The boner's eyes are gone and its remaining skin is black because of necrosis. A boner has very little inspiration to move from its nest unless it is provoked by approaching stimuli. Therefore, when a non-infected human stumbles upon a boner, the zombie will instinctively attack it in order to spread its disease.

- <u>Stage 5: Skeletal</u>. There comes a point after all of the zombie's flesh is gone in which there is no possible way for the zombie to move itself. There is only a frame with no tendons, muscle, or flesh of any kind. The framer's brain may be functional as it continues to operate through a viral infection, but it has nothing to animate, making the zombie harmless, except for the brain matter itself, which is still contagious.

Note: To get a better picture of what a "boner" might look like, watch the movie *Warm Bodies*, which provides numerous examples of what it calls "bonies".

Zombie Mobility

There are various ways in which zombies roam the world and attack non-infected humans. Since they are operating as the living dead, they will function and give chase until their brain has been decommissioned. Therefore, removing a zombie's legs or other limbs is not a means to dispose of them or keep them from chasing you. Involuntarily, they will follow you until you are far from their sight, regardless of the shape of their bodies.

- <u>Walkers</u>. Walking is the typical mode of mobility for the living dead. Walkers are easy to escape from because a non-infected person can jog away from them. However, walkers do form groups, and often surround their victims, making escape more difficult. In addition, since walkers move slowly, they can sneak up on their prey, and they are nearly indestructible in hand-to-hand combat situations, so their intended target is certain to become infected once they are in a walker's grip. Depending on the state of decay and the overall condition of the zombie's body, walkers may twitch as they move, walk with a stumbling gate because of muscle stiffness, or drag a crushed or broken leg as they slide along.

- <u>Runners</u>. are zombies with the capability to run at a full sprint without ever losing energy. There is no way to outrun these sprinters because they never slow down, so you better be prepared to attack them with some form of weaponry to disorient them, remove their legs, or dispose of them before they reach you.

- <u>Stalkers</u>. These zombies walk on all fours and are mutated to the point of heavy devolution. They take on the form of a primitive animal from their previously human self. Their peculiar means of mobility provides them with cover in tall vegetation, and their use of all four limbs to propel themselves provides stalkers with additional speed, so they can come at their victims unseen and in a hurry.

- <u>Crawlers</u>. These injured zombies do not have the means to walk upright and give chase because they don't' have the means to do so. Either their legs have rotted to the point that their bones can no longer carry them, or they have been damaged in some fashion. Damage to the zombie's legs could have occurred in a number of ways: Their shanks could have been severed in some fashion, crushed by a falling object or a moving car, or they were blown away by a weapon or severely injured during battle. People might think you are safe from these zombies, but they move unsuspectedly below their prey's knee level and often bite ankles, which are why they are called "ankle biters". They can also fit nicely into crawl spaces, under beds, and other place one might not normally suspect to find the "walking" dead.

Note: For a better understanding of "runners", watch the film World War Z. In the movie, the zombies are agile and fast with the sole purpose of infecting—not eating—the uninfected, which occurs in an amazing 12 seconds. When there is no prey in the area, they go dormant, and lose their coordination and speed, but rev up into high gear when new flesh arrives.

Zombie Hunting Traits

While the intelligence of zombies is low-level and nearly non-existent, their hunting instincts do improve after they move from human to beast. Zombies are more keen to sights, sounds, and smells, like an animal, and they are only equipped with a basic instinct to survive, and in order to do that, they are required to eat flesh, which spreads their pathogen. In most designs of zombies, the unfortunate thing for them is that while their senses improve, their physicality does not. In other words, their deteriorating body does not allow for agility and quickness like most wildlife. With the exception of the "runner", zombies only have a few tactics available for finding their next victim.

- <u>Lurkers</u>. Lurkers conserve their energy and expel it only when they are on the attack. The zombies do not hunt for prey. Instead, they hide In the shadows of vacated structures or in the weeds, bushes, and caves of the outdoors until a victim approaches. These slackers go dormant while they wait on an uninfected human to show up, and it is only then that they spring to life to snatch their victim.

- <u>Roamers</u>. Roamers sniff out prey. They follow sights, sounds, and smells in order to seek out a victim. They do not have the patience to wait for prey to arrive at their doorstep. Instead, they are in constant motion, and often roam around the gates of places where they know the uninfected congregate. Some have the ability to climb walls in order to find possible targets for their infection, but usually they do not understand how to make their way past any standing structure, door, or gate.

- Packers. Sometimes, a group of zombies will form, but it isn't intentional. Packs of zombies are drawn together by the possibility of potential prey. In other words, like a wake of vultures, they wander in the same directions in order to meet potential meals, not to socialize with one another. However, it does hinder their hunt, but they aren't intelligent enough to understand that is the case. The obvious hindrances are that groups of zombies are easier to spot and hear, and large groups attacking single individuals is not a productive use of resources. Some zombie experts theorize that a zombie's pack mentality is derived from a dormant consciousness that drives them to form "social" groups.

- <u>Nesters</u>. Nesters are lurkers, who live in dark corridors with other zombies. Like roaming groups of zombies, there is nothing intentional about the action of zombies forming what looks to be a coven. It is only a matter of convenience. Presumably, as lurkers turn humans to zombies, those zombies stay within the nest, waiting out their next victim together. As the victims grow in numbers, so does the size of the nest.

Zombie Capabilities

Zombies have bizarre capabilities that assist them in claiming victims while on the prowl for human flesh. Since their brains have become mush, they don't have the intelligence—in most cases—to make a weapon or use one, so instead they rely on that talents that their viral infection allows.

- <u>Goliath Zombies</u>. Like the Hulk of comic book fame, Goliath zombies have super human strength that allows them to pick up large objects and toss them at their victim and pull off chunks of buildings to throw at their targets. They can also crush and stomp their prey into submission before infecting them with a bite.

- <u>Exploders and Bursters</u>. Exploders can detonate themselves like a shrapnel grenade—a form of suicide or self-destruction—in order to spread their pathogen. In other cases, exploders, a form of bloater, erupt when attacked by a sharp weapon that opens them up. In both cases, built-up internal gases cause them to detonate. Exploders, sometimes called bursters, can take out a victim with a combination of bone fragments, which open up wounds, and infectious body tissue and fluids that walk right into those gashes.

- <u>Pukers and Spitters</u>. Accompanying puking zombies, you will often hear belching, which provides some warning that they are near. This type of zombie will either drop a load of vomit from a location above you, like a rooftop or balcony, or can violently project a smoking round of puke. If the vomit is ingested by a non-infected human, or it makes contact with an open wound, the person will become infected. Since pukers are constantly throwing up, they are limited in energy and are covered in a vile concoction of vomited body fluids. Much like pukers, spitters can project a toxic mix of disease or acid at their victims. While pukers normally vomit involuntarily, spitters have control of the liquid in their decaying bowels, and can produce it and propel at will. In many cases, the acid in the spit opens a wound, which allows the accompanying infection to infiltrate a victim's system and infect their cells.

- <u>Floaters and Water Walkers</u>. Floaters are a type of zombie that end up in the water. These zombies were forced off a boat or drowned, and now float around waiting for their next victim. Floaters are "bloaters", using the gas within them to stay above the waterline. Once the gas is gone from their bodies, there is a single option left: to walk below the surface of the water. Zombies do not have the intelligence to doggy paddle or swim, so they sink, and can walk to the nearest shore, though it might take some time, considering the underwater obstacles and tides they will have to overcome.

- <u>Spiders</u>. Some zombies evolve some of the characteristics of the parasite that infected them.

In some cases, hundreds of thousands of small hairs develop on the zombie's hands and feet, like those found on most insects. These hairs, called setules, allow the zombies to crawl up walls and hang on ceilings. So-called spider zombies do not attack unless provoked. Their only objective is to roost in places where they cannot be found in order to allow the parasites within them to grow and hatch. Once the parasites are born, they burst from the host zombie's body in search of a new home by infecting raw meat and contaminating water supplies, while waiting for the ingestion of the infected source. If these zombies are cornered or feel threatened, they will attack and kill their victim.

- Evolvers. Zombies with the ability to adapt to their environment, and gain intelligence over a period of time are called evolvers. As the cells of these zombies rejuvenate, they become physically faster and stronger. Along with the rejuvenation of their physicality, their minds begin to develop as brain cells roar back to life with new zeal. Over time, they begin to drink water, eat for nutrients, while hunting down prey in order to spread their infection. In some cases, memories form, but the zombies never fully develop the ability to understand them or regain empathy. However, there is obvious conflict and struggle within them, and lack of focus sometimes jeopardizes their instincts to maim and infect. This small disadvantage does not override the clear advantages such as speed, agility, and the ability to climb walls, open doors, and perform tactical maneuvers like stalking and ambushes.

Note: One of the earliest accounts of zombies can be found in the story Epic of Gilgamesh. The Mesopotamian folk tale that is more than 4,000 years old tells the story of the goddess Ishtar, who threatened to raise the dead to consume the living in a fit of rage against humankind.

Zombie Senses

Zombies transition from human omnivores, which eat a combination of meats and vegetation, to full-on carnivores with one desire: flesh. When this evolution occurs, they become instinctive beats that rely on their basic senses to find their desired targets. Zombie experts say that a zombie virus disrupts neurons that regulate satiety, or hunger. For a zombie, hunger is never quenched, and because of it, the senses that humans take for granted and seldom use for survival, become hypersensitive.

There is no more important sense for a zombie than smell. A zombie's eyes might dissolve to nothing like the rest of their flesh, and their hearing might disappear as well because the eardrum is a delicate instrument that could fall to decay. Their sense of taste is unimportant because a zombie is not looking for a particular flavor to quench its appetite because they are always hungry, and presumably, the tongue and its taste buds would dissolve over time. A zombie's sense of smell is everything, even as their nose falls from their face. They are able to decipher between the smell of fresh meat and the rotting flesh of their fellow zombies, and as a shark is drawn to the smallest trickle of blood in the water, a zombie can pick up the smell of the body's red juice from long distances. Wounded humans are the most susceptible to a zombie stalking, but the general smell of an uninfected human instinctively forces a zombie into action.

There is science behind the notion that the sense of smell becomes more powerful. A study published in *The Journal of Neuroscience* in 2012 titled "Altered Cross-Modal Processing" reported that the brain rewires itself for survival when one or more of the five senses is disabled. For example, people who are born deaf use areas of the brain that are typically reserved for sound to process advanced levels of sight and touch. Beyond that, it is believed that deaf people experience a higher level of sight that extends to a "perceptual illusion" that people with normal hearing wouldn't even understand from a conceptual point of view. The same thing occurs to zombies as their sense of sight, sound, and taste diminishes; their sense of smell improves, during the middles stages of infection.

As a zombie rots, their eyeballs begin to decay, reducing their ability to see, as has been noted. While they can trace scents because of their enhanced sense of smell, reduced vision and even touch and hearing make it difficult for them to maneuver around objects and follow paths. Therefore, in some instances, "echolocation" evolves to replace the missing senses. Echolocation, also called bio sonar, is used by numerous species of animals to navigate and forage, most notably bats and dolphins. These animals, and some zombies, issue a "call" that bounces off surrounding objects, and paints a picture of their surroundings. In most cases, the zombies use a clicking noise to measure the distance to objects and the dimensions of them to assist with moving around obstacles and along paths to find their way to the next victim.

Zombie Language

Zombies do communicate, even though it is greatly muted by their devolution. The main form of communication is an ongoing expression of pain. They moan and groan with each agonizing step they take. Either a zombie's grunts are a response to the physical difficulty of each plunge forward, or it is an expression of the mental difficulty they encounter in a world they do not understand. Their basic language is left over from their former human self, in which they are attempting to display some form of grief, but "groaning" is the extent of their offering of communication. They don't even have the mental capacity or desire to motion or use basic sign language, such as pointing.

Types of Zombie Infections

- Parasitic Zombies. As we have discussed in detail, these types of zombies are carriers and transmitters of a zombie virus. These zombies could be a shell filled with parasites, which are waiting to escape their body in order to find a new host, produce larvae, and nest and incubate a new swarm of parasites. The parasites take over the mind of their host, positioning them into scenarios that benefit their incubation and eventual release.

- Fungal Zombies. We have discussed *Ophiocordyceps unilateralis*, which infects Thai ants through the inhalation of spores, making it zombie-like and bringing it to its death. The same thing occurs to humans who inhale a zombie fungus spore. The fungus takes over the victim's central nervous system, directing it to a dark and damp location in order for the fungus to grow more rapidly. Eventually, the fungus takes over the body while it is alive, but powerless to do anything, pushing out in stalks from easily accessible orifices, usually the eye sockets since the spores normally grow in the sinus cavities. In cases in which the spores enter the digestives system, stalks can sometimes sprout from the anus. The zombie is then compelled by the fungus to find a high place in order for the spores to catch the wind and fall below to unsuspecting victims.

- Viral Zombies. The zombie could have a virus that is spread through the transfer of body fluids. The fluids excrete from the open wounds of the infected, are evident on fingernails, which now act as claws and virus-delivering devices, and reside in their mouth and on their teeth. Once the zombie makes contact with the body fluid of an uninfected human through a membrane or open wound, it moves quickly to the cells of the central nervous system, and the victim immediately become a member of the living dead.

- <u>Atomic Zombies</u>. Through direct contact with radiation because of the melt down of a nuclear power plant, exposure to high quantities of atomic energy, or during an accident at a biochemical manufacturing plant, these zombies might act erratically, but are not normally aggressive. Contact with the zombie can contaminate non-infected individuals, but there are other possibilities for transmission because atomic zombies can contaminate water sources and food supplies.

- <u>Voodoo Zombies</u>. As it has been told, a voodoo zombie is an actual reality in Haiti and other Caribbean cultures where witch doctors are still a part of common human culture. Sorcerers can also be found in Romania, France, New Orleans, and within traveling bands of gypsies across the world. Voodoo zombies are in some form of trance, which can be permanent if caused by a potion containing toxins, but they can also be under a spell, a state of hypnosis, which can be broken in some cases. Since these types of zombies are not infected by a pathogen or parasite, they aren't aggressive against all of humanity. They can sometimes be ordered to do devious things by their controller, but they do not have the capability to spread their zombie-state by passing along an infection of some sort.

Note: In Hindu mythology, a vetala is a spirit that invades the body of a corpse, and uses it to torment the living in a hostile manner. These demons, who are locked in purgatory because they did not receive funerary rights, have enhanced power, feed on human blood, and have a venom that causes paralysis. Their tricks on humans lead them to madness and cause miscarriages.

Section 3:

How to Survive the Zombie Apocalypse

Throughout world history, we find zombies, and currently, there are two ongoing zombie viruses that are being studied: the Necro-Mortosis virus and the 29ID-HHQ virus. The governments of the world do not want to alarm their populaces because they wish to control us. They understand that the reality of a viral apocalypse will create mass hysteria, and they would lose control of their governing powers if the world was nearing its end. Therefore, it is up to the normal, everyday citizens of the world to spread the word about the impending apocalypse. It is up to us individuals to prepare ourselves and our families for the moment of doom when a zombie virus travels at such a horrific speed across the planet that zombies outnumber humans in only a few short days, weeks, or months. We must be vigilant in order to stay alive, strike zombies from existence, and save humanity from extinction.

Day Zero

When the zombie pandemic becomes our lives, governments will dismantle, social orders will dissipate, borders will disappear, money will have no value and mean nothing, and life will become very different. Those people with unlimited resources and high positions in government will have secure bunkers, and food and water supplies to keep them alive for months. The rest of us will be on our own.

Bands of criminals will loot stores at will as police forces evaporate in order to secure their own survival. Our armed military forces will disband as well. There will be no one to protect us. In fact, military and police personnel, equipped with weapons and protective gear, may become bandits in order to save themselves and provide for their families. Therefore, we will be on our own fighting zombies, the elements, and other humans who want to take the resources we have found to survive.

Transportation networks will be gone, and evacuated vehicles will line highways and roads, making it difficult to escape big cities. Electricity will die, technology will fade away, and communication will return to its basic forms. You will not have a mobile phone, you will not have access to news reports, and you will not know the ongoing condition of the rest of the world.

Food supplies will grow thin, and there will be no one to transport new supplies to local markets. Fresh water will be difficult to find. Caged and penned livestock will perish. Unmanned crops will die.

Zombies will destroy the inner cities, and the suburbs will quickly become wastelands as zombies move from urban areas to neighboring suburban ones to find new blood. The "living" will flock to the countryside to escape, but the "dead" will arrive in the rural areas in time, looking for fresh humans to infect.

There will be those that give up as the apocalypse begins, and do not resist. They will take what they can, live in decadence their final days, and disappear into the face of a zombie. These people who refuse to fight for their lives will be the living dead that you will eventually have to fight to survive. They're better of dead, really, because they are of no use to anyone. Although, many people who give it their best shot at living through the apocalypse will melt away as well. Trapped behind walls, their minds will become polluted by despair. They will commit suicide or go out in a blaze of glory, entering the streets and taking out as many zombies as possible until they run out of ammunition and fade into the darkness of a zombie-state.

However, you will never give up hope. You will never accept your fate to become a zombie. No, you are a hopeful warrior, a survivor, and that is why you are reading this handbook.

Though, there will be dark days for you as well.

While an independent army of zombies ravishes the world without the need for a re-supply of water, food, shelter, or ammunition, an uninfected human needs all of those things to survive. There are also the emotional aspects of a zombie virus. Zombies do not have to deal with corrupt relationships, poor leadership within a group, the death of friends and family, PTSD, or low morale. Humans do. We, the last of our race, will feel pain in the physical form, feel agony from emotional distress, feel heartbreak, feel anguish, and feel mental instability creeping upon us. We must stay strong through it all.

The key to surviving is to settle.

It may not be in our nature anymore to find a spot and stay there without luxury, but we must. We currently live in a fast moving society. We can get to places quickly. We can get news immediately. However, the main ingredient for survival in a world filled with zombies is the understanding that your previous life is gone, along with all of your fancy gadgets, your easy modes of transport, your delicious meals, your favorite restaurants, your local bar or club, your concerts and movie nights. They will be all be gone, and rapid adaptation to a life without possessions, social scenes and structures, and ease of movement, will be a part of your new life.

It will become immediately necessary for you to think of yourself as an indigenous citizen of your land, or as an early pioneer of your landscape, for you have to settle, limit your movement and involvement in the world until better times arrive. Beyond zombies, there will be bands of thieves and murderers who you must outsmart and outmaneuver in the beginning days, but those marauders will never settle, and that will be their downfall. They will be eaten up by the world, and more literally, by zombies. You and your nest of people will be safe. However, even if you find yourself alone, you must maintain your sanity in order to survive, or you may never find your people, or some people, to form a colony.

For the most part, you must forget about nationalism and localism, about the governments and borders that once bound you. You are on your own. Hopefully, you will be with a loved one, but that isn't a given, and while you might feel compelled to look for them, it is a bad idea. The only way to get to them is to be rational. It is fine to dream of the reunion if it helps you to keep hope alive, but it should not drive you to make bad decisions to get to them sooner than it is possible.

Your life will consist of deconstructed landscapes of burned cities, the stench of rot and decay, and abandoned homes and vehicles. The remains of corpuses will outline the paths you follow, silent atmospheres will be snapped into intensity at the slightest noise that comes from the unrest of the moans of zombies, the screams of their victims, and any operating, motorized vehicle that could be carrying a human scavenger who will take your goods and eat your heart.

Stop, and really consider a zombie world, because all of the mentioned things will be your life, and that life is on its way. An outbreak or two is a part of our current world, and the following steps are what you must follow to survive, steps that must be taken starting now, this very day, "Day Zero". We are currently in "Stage 1" of the zombie apocalypse, and there are only four stages:

- Stage 1 consists of the early hours in a zombie apocalypse. A small pocket, or two, of a zombie infection exists, consisting of less than 100 reported cases at one time. We are in this stage. We are always in this stage because we do not know what is occurring in every outpost around the world, in the jungles, in the slums, in places where everyday people go. News reports regarding "cannibalism", "mysterious attacks", a "rash of murders", and "contained virus" are signs of impending doom.

- Stage 2 may take a month to reach its full potential as a hundred victims of a "mysterious virus" turn to a thousand of them. Small pockets of zombie activity will turn into regional concerns. When this level is reached, it will dominate news reports, and hysteria will begin.

- Stage 3 is several months down the road from stage 2, as zombies dominate all news matters and daily life in the world. A large region will be dismantled by the presence of zombies, and the quarantine of travelers who are suspected of carrying the disease will be a regular item of concern as countries attempt to keep the virus from spreading to their shores. At some point, all travel between nations will cease, and possibly, air travel within nations will discontinue as well.

- Stage 4 is the apocalypse. If you make it to stage 4 it is only because you read this book and prepared yourself for this worst case scenario.

Preparing for the Zombie Apocalypse from Stage 1 to 4

You must be prepared for every stage of the zombie apocalypse, with "Stage 1" preparation being the most important. Without pre-planning, you will begin the later stages in full panic mode, presumably becoming a pirate in the world, continually scavenging for food, water, and supplies. This is no way to live, and an impossible way to survive a world dominated by the dead.

Stage 1: Preparation

Forming a Team or Partnership

There is no room on your collected team for anyone who you don't trust. Acquaintances are not acceptable members regardless of their charm, strength, intelligence, survival expertise, adaptability, or even suspected honesty. None of that matters. Will the people on your team remain loyal because of the years you have spent together with them? Have they ever let you down? If they have broken trust and disappointed you in a major way, do you expect to maintain their loyalty in an adverse situation? You need to find a team or a partnership with people who will have your back, and would die before they killed you for your resources. Find people who share with your, have helped you in a difficult real world situation, someone you could sleep next to, and not worry that your throat might be cut when the food runs out.

In the same sense, find someone who trusts you in the same manner. If you are teamed with members who are not confident in you, they will put you in jeopardy by taking risks because they do not feel that you can protect them on night guard, forage and hunt with them to find food, or make it to the end with them. They might leave you behind or put you in danger, not because they are bad people, but because they don't feel you can keep up or hold your end of the bargain. The loyalty and the trust of everyone on your team must extend all ways.

You will have to make difficult decisions when putting together your zombie-apocalypse team or partnership if you hope to survive, and that is something you need to come to terms with now. Protecting an old person with limited mobility will get you killed. Taking care of a small child who cannot protect themself will get you killed. It is OK if you are unwilling to leave loved ones behind who are too old or too young to survive, but understand that survival will become more difficult if you have to manage yourself and another person. Those who survive the zombie apocalypse will be among the smartest in the world, the bravest in the world, the most emotionally fit people in the world, the most adaptable and savvy people in the world, and they will also be agile and physically fit. The people on your team must meet those requirements to improve your chances of survival.

In addition, Pets do not go with you. They are unpredictable, they make noise, and they require food and water that will be in short supply. Sorry, you will not survive with them in your possession.

Survival Training

This is a zombie survival handbook, a guide designed to assist you in surviving a zombie apocalypse. It will help you greatly in understanding the impact of a virus on the world and the capabilities of a zombie; and soon, this book will teach you basic survival skills. However, you will need other survival manuals, and you need to own those books now, and when you are deciding whether to pack your Harry Potter books or your survival guides, the choice is an obvious one. You need to know how to survive in the wilderness, you will need a guide that details what plants are edible, what animals are dangerous, how to make hunting traps and fishing lures, how to procure safe drinking water, find natural medicines, apply first aid to wounds, and make zombie alarms. You will need to know how to make a bow and arrows, how to shoot a gun, and basic hand-to-hand combat techniques.

Logistical Preparation

You must have a plan for evacuation if you get caught in an apocalyptic zombie storm. You need to be vigilant, though, and get out early. While, you may have a bunker, a basement, or some sort of shelter filled with luxuries, food, water, and supplies to last a decade, you will not survive the first month of Stage 4 if you remain there. If your fortress is in an urban environment, you are toast within a day. If it is in the suburbs, zombies and bandits will overrun you within days. Fighting will be in the streets and all around your house. If there is military of any kind left, they will be bombarding the inner city and connecting suburbs to kill zombies. There might be warning of an attack, but how will you evacuate? You will be stuck and you will be corpse in a crater.

Rural areas will survive Stage 4 for a time, so escape from there is possible, but you don't want to remain there unless it is secluded, and not a settlement of numerous homes. While rural areas may not be as dense as the city and suburbs, if is still unsafe for long-term survival. The zombies go where the people go, and there will be millions of the living dead who will smell out your flesh and eat you alive. If they don't find you, the looters will. In the end, it will be rough, and those bandits will come to rape and pillage, literally. It might be your friendly neighbor who is desperate and depraved, and takes it out on you. It might be the kid who mows your lawn. It could be anyone, so trust no one except those you have chosen to be a part of your team, and get to the wilderness as fast as you can.

With your stockpile of goods, get to a desolate location, and then keep going. You need to get to a place with no roads and no power lines. Do not go to a state or national park. While it is technically the wilderness in some locations, others survivors will be there because it seems practical and familiar, and it is the "easy" thing to do. However, it is not far enough from civilization, and you will not survive there. Those parks are danger zones where marauders will show up. Go off the main roads, and even dirt roads, and we will tell you how to survive once you get there.

Finding a New Home during the Zombie Apocalypse

Scout your wilderness location during Stage 1. Do not wing it in Stage 2 or 3. Find three suitable locations that you can get to in a hurry, and visit them beforehand. You are not trying to decide upon one suitable place between three locations; you are trying to find three locations that are suitable because you need options, depending on the season you are leaving and depending on the routes out of town. Consider the harsh conditions you might encounter in each location. Will you be able to survive a blistering summer or an unbearable winter there? Is there enough food for survival for several years? These things must be considered.

Buy the land that you find if possible. Build a cabin there if you can. Spend time on the property. If you don't have the resources to purchase the property, then do not fret, just make sure you spend some nights there in a primitive way to see if you can survive off the land. Buy books that detail the region, its weather, and resources, and have maps of the area.

The following are prerequisites for your zombie apocalypse landing spot:

- Getting to your new home should follow a route that "isn't" easy, because it shouldn't be a piece of cake to get to any of the three locations you choose, but is shouldn't be impossible. You should consider that all public travel will be suspended, so the likelihood of getting to an island or anywhere on the other side of a large body of water will not be possible.

- Your haven of humanity needs to be 500 miles from all human life.

- Your domicile of promise needs to have a natural line of defense, such as a river boundary, high altitude, a canopy above you, and camouflage all around.

- Your sanctuary of zombie defiance will need trees, so that you have wood to make fires and to construct a shelter.

- Your fortress of faith needs to be located near fresh water supplies, and presumably, it will be since it is 500 miles away from civilization. Just make sure it isn't located in the desert.

- Your homestead of hope needs to be in an area that has food.

  - Are there animals to hunt?
  - Are there fish to be caught?
  - Is the soil cultivatable?
  - Is there food for foraging? You will be eating all that is available, and your headquarters should have wild vegetables, berries, and other edible vegetation.

- If you get there, and it is overrun with zombies, head to Site B, and then Site C if possible. Remember, choose three spots, and have a backup plan if one becomes unavailable.

Required Gear

The comprehensive list of gear that follows will be needed for every individual on your team. It is a requirement because seriously bad things happen during a zombie apocalypse: teams become separated, team members die, and retrieval of their gear will be next to impossible in most scenarios. You may never make it to your wilderness location, you might not have transportation, or a route out of town, and you might find yourself alone. Therefore, in any survival situation that you wish to survive, you will need all of the "required" gear that is listed to get through a night, a week, a month, or the rest of your life while zombies are on the prowl.

All of the gear on the list should be stashed in a 70-110 liter backpack. These packs, called expedition or mountaineering packs, are big enough to accommodate necessities for at least a week, so a re-supply of food and water will be necessary.

List of main necessities:

- Navigation

  o Map (with protective case)
  o Compass

- Sun protection

  o Sunscreen
  o Lip balm
  o Sunglasses

- Backpacking boots that wrap way above your upper ankle and have stiff midsoles that provide ultimate support for hiking through wilderness terrain in extreme conditions, and for stomping zombies.

- Warm weather clothing

  o Wicking T-shirt (synthetic or wool)
  o Wicking underwear
  o Quick-drying pants or shorts
  o Long-sleeve shirt (for sun, bugs)
  o Sun-shielding hat
  o Bandana or Buff
  o Rainwear (jacket, pants)
  o Socks (synthetic or wool) plus spares

- Cold weather clothing

  o Wicking long-sleeve T-shirt
  o Wicking long underwear (good sleepwear)
  o Beanie
  o Gloves
  o Rainwear (jacket, pants)
  o Soft shell jacket
  o Socks (synthetic or wool) plus spares

- Nutritious meals and cooking supplies

  o Ample food supply
  o Stove
  o Fuel
  o Cooking set (with pot grabber)
  o Dishes or bowls
  o Utensils
  o Collapsible cup

- Hydration

  o Water bottles or hydration reservoirs
  o Water filter or other treatment system
  o Cistern for collecting rain water

- Illumination

  o Headlamp or flashlight
  o Collapsible solar lantern
  o Extra batteries

- Fire

  o Matches or lighter
  o Waterproof container
  o Fire starter (for emergency survival fire)

- Knife, preferably multi-tool

- Toiletry

- Toilet paper

- Camping Gear

  o Tent or hammock
  o Sleeping bag
  o Sleeping pad

List of first-aid supplies and emergency items:

- Antiseptic wipes (BZK-based wipes preferred; alcohol-based OK)
- Antibacterial ointment (e.g., bacitracin)
- Compound tincture of benzoin (bandage adhesive)
- Assorted adhesive bandages (fabric preferred)
- Butterfly bandages / adhesive wound-closure strips
- Gauze pads (various sizes)
- Nonstick sterile pads
- Medical adhesive tape (10 yd. roll, min. 1" width)
- Blister treatment
- Ibuprofen / other pain-relief medication
- Insect sting relief treatment
- Antihistamine to treat allergic reactions
- Splinter (fine-point) tweezers
- Safety pins
- First-aid manual or information cards

Wraps, Splints and Wound Coverings

- Elastic wrap
- Triangular cravat bandage
- Finger splint(s)
- SAM splint(s)
- Rolled gauze
- Rolled, stretch-to-conform bandages
- Hydrogel-based pads
- First-aid cleansing pads with topical anesthetic
- Hemostatic (blood-stopping) gauze
- Liquid bandage

- Oval eye pads

Medications/Treatments

- Hand sanitizer (BKZ- or alcohol-based)
- Aloe vera gel (sun exposure relief)
- Aspirin (primarily for response to a heart attack)
- Antacid tablets
- Throat lozenges
- Lubricating eye drops
- Loperamide tablets (for diarrhea symptoms)
- Poison ivy / poison oak treatment
- Insect sting relief treatment
- Glucose or other sugar to treat hypoglycemia
- Oral rehydration salts
- Antifungal foot powder
- Prescription medications (e.g., antibiotics)
- Injectable epinephrine to treat allergic reactions

Suggested Tools and Supplies

- Paramedic shears (blunt-tip scissors)
- Safety razor blade (or scalpel w/ #15 or #12 blade)
- Cotton-tipped swabs
- Standard oral thermometer
- Low-reading (hypothermia) thermometer
- Irrigation syringe with 18-gauge catheter
- Magnifying glass
- Small mirror
- Medical / surgical gloves (nitrile preferred; avoid latex)

- CPR mask
- Steel sewing needle with heavy-duty thread
- Needle-nose pliers with wire cutter
- Duct tape (small roll)
- Small notepad with waterproof pencil or pen
- Medical waste bag (plus box for sharp items)
- Waterproof container to hold supplies and meds
- Emergency heat-reflecting blanket
- Headlamp (preferred) or flashlight
- Whistle (pealess preferred)
- Personal locator beacon
- Satellite messenger

Suggested Personal Care, Other Items

- Insect repellent (plus headnet, if needed)
- Hand sanitizer
- Biodegradable soap
- Water-treatment chemicals
- Collapsible water sink or basin

Food

It is best to pack food that does not require cooking. Camp stoves malfunction at times and fires attract the attention of looters and zombies, and you'll be left with less to eat if you bring items that need to be cooked with no way to cook them. If you can't do without hot food, make sure you have the fuel required to heat them. Freeze-dried meals only need boiling water, but items like pasta, rice, and potatoes, take a long time to cook. Also, keep in mind that fresh food has a short lifespan, and canned foods are heavy. Pack food that is lightweight and not bulky.

Food Ideas for Each Meal:

- Breakfast options: Instant oatmeal, grits, dry cereal, breakfast bars, dehydrated eggs, pancake mix, fresh fruit.

- Lunch options: Energy bars, dried fruit, nuts, seeds, bagels, tortillas, hard cheese, peanut butter, jerky.

- Supper options: Packaged, freeze-dried meals, dried vegetables, lentils, instant soup, instant rice, instant potatoes, tuna, salami, pasta.

Water

Water is priority number one during a zombie apocalypse. Hot or cold, high or low altitude, there is nothing more important than staying hydrated. Your level of water intake depends on some key factors and involves climate, altitude, physical difficulty, and availability of water from natural sources or watering stations.

Hot or humid conditions require one or more quarts of water per hour while on the move by foot, and even though the air is cooler at high elevations, don't be fooled; the air is thinner and drier at higher altitudes and it dehydrates people faster than at sea-level.

Water Sources

Finding water sources is a key to survival. It is important to do research of the area where you will be located in order to verify viable waters sources. A map will help, but water sources dry up, so prior reconnaissance of the area is important. The safest water comes from a "trickling" source. It needs to be moving through rocks and roots, which clears it of many solids. However, it is essential to purify water from all sources that you come across if possible. Drink mixes help the taste of natural sources and bitter purifying chemicals.

Water Sources to Avoid:

- Standing puddles, animal troughs, or small ponds where there is no flow of water.

- Beaver ponds, which are often associated with the parasite giardia.

- Water directly under a waterfall or cascade, or water bar or interceptor dyke, because it will contain more solids that are harder to purify.

- Rivers downstream from a city or industrial area, or animal pasture or cultivated field.

- Any water source that is foamy, orange or red-colored, or has animal feces on the shoreline.

Purifying Drinking Water:

- The best way to purify drinking water is to boil it before you drink it. Boiling water kills bacteria, protozoa, and viruses. To properly purify the water, heat it until it comes to a rolling boil for one minute at low altitudes and three minutes at elevations above 2,000 meters (6,5601 feet). Boiling water will require you to bring a small camping stove.

- Purification tablets are light and the chemicals in the tablets destroy dangerous parasites. Once the chemical settles for at least 30 minutes, the chlorine dioxide in the tablets neutralize giardia, and four hours for cryptosporidium, so plan accordingly.

- Ultraviolet light purifiers destroy bacteria, protozoa and viruses as you stir the water with the purifier. After 90 seconds, the UV rays make the water safe to drink.

- Sip or squeeze water filters, pump water filters, and gravity water filters can also purify water through a filtration process that involves microscopic pores. These devices filter out bacteria and protozoa, but usually not viruses.

Weapons and Protective Gear

You will need numerous weapons at your disposal. If you find yourself on foot, you will only be able to take a few with you, but it is important to have an arsenal for all possibilities you might encounter if you are stuck somewhere in the middle stages of the zombie apocalypse and have to fight your way out of it.

Weapons:

- Long fixed blade knife with a partially serrated edge, which can be used as a pommel or spear, and a sheath with a built-in blade sharpener

- Dual multi-function folding knife with a partially serrated edge and a striking pommel

- Compact fixed knife with a partially serrated edge, blunt tip, a bottle opener, a pocket clip, and a locking sheath.

- 18-inch dual purpose machete with a saw on one side and a chopping blade on the other with a nylon sheath.

- Multi-purpose machete that is fashioned to chop, gather, cut, dig, or sharpen with a military-grade sheath.

- Parang machete with an angled blade for clearing vegetation with a nylon sheath.

- Compact axe with a long handle and a forged steel head that houses a coarse blade handsaw within the handle.

- Tactical Crossbow that has red dot sight, scope, and an LED flashlight with a carrying case.

- Long utility, wrecking Bar, which is basically a high-speed hammer that can crush a skull, and be used to pull out nails, demolish doors, open bottles, and chisel.

- Pump-action shotgun, which is a practical way to kill zombies when your crossbow arrows run out, and there are too many zombies to attack with a machete or axe.

- 9 mm pistol with a silencer, for emergencies within close range of an attacker.

- Rifle with a silencer.

- Unbreakable, polypropylene baseball bat, for last resort close encounters.

- 500 rounds of rifle bullets, 500 shotgun shells, 500 pistol rounds, and 250 crossbow bolts (reusable in some cases).

Protective Gear:

- Heavy duty Kevlar tactical gloves with hard shell plates to protect the back of your hands.

- Protective racing jacket with high-impact, two-piece chest plate, and back, elbow, and shoulder coverage.

- Lightweight Kevlar helmet with mask and drape.

Other Gear:

- Thermal eye camera, which detects heat signatures up to 1,000 feet away in total darkness or heavy smoke, and is waterproof and shock resistant, for night watch.

- Binoculars, which enable at least 8X magnification, and are fog and waterproof, for spotting zombies or friendly folks from a distance while on guard.

- Professional bump key set, which, with some moderate training, allows you to open the majority of locks you will encounter to find supplies and seek coverage as you travel.

- Rechargeable, battery powered, shortwave radio.

Vehicle

You will need a vehicle, and you will need to get out of the city with it before mass hysteria makes it impossible to travel on roads and highways. Traffic gridlock will lead to the abandonment of vehicles, which will provide obstacles that cannot breached, and then you will be traveling by foot, skirting highways and roads with little protection from zombies and bandits, a heavy backpack, and a limited supply of food and water. You do not want to find yourself in this position. You need to be on the road and headed to your clandestine new home before Stage 3.

Also, consider the necessity for gas to get you to you across the country to the wilderness. Plan the places you will stop to get gas and supplies if needed. You will need a fuel efficient SUV with all-terrain features, so that can advance down dirt roads and across difficult terrain during this time, so ensure that someone on your assembled team or your partner has one. An SUV gives you ample space for two people and all of your supplies, but not much more. In other words, your team will need one SUV for every two people. There will come a point when the vehicle will need to be abandoned and a hike of some distance will commence, but you will want to get as close to your destination and across some difficult terrain before you leave your vehicle to trek a few hundred miles trough the wilderness to your final location.

Combat Training

While hand-to-hand combat should be avoided with anyone, living or dead, you must be prepared for any situation that settles upon you, so it is important to train in self-defense and be physically fit in order to free yourself from the grip of your opponent, before you create some distance and pull out a weapon. Do not fool yourself into thinking that you will be able to survive a zombie apocalypse if you are a heavy smoker, overweight, or have no cardiovascular fitness. You need to be in excellent shape, and have the stamina to walk many miles, and the ability to sprint for minutes at a time. You will need to be able to carry heavy weaponry and a large backpack across steep and unforgiving terrain.

You will need to go to a gun range and learn how to shoot all your weapons and hit targets, so that you will be able to hit zombies between the eyes. You will need to learn how to use your crossbow, how to swing a machete and axe. Familiarization with all of these things is crucial in order for it to become second nature. You do not want to have any reservations when the day comes when you must shoot down a zombie or a human predator, and remember those zombies and human predators may have once been your friend or family member. They may have even been someone you loved dearly, but in all cases you must end their life if they attack you in the living form, or end their misery if they are of the dead variety.

Stage 2: Evacuation

If you want to greatly increase your chances of survival, then you best be getting down the road when the zombie virus reaches Stage 2. There is no time to ponder the idea because things begin to fall apart in this stage. You need to be in your new wilderness home before stage 3 arrives, which is when the unprepared will visit the realm of the living dead.

Vehicular Escape

Load up the car, and prepare for a life of vigilance with your team or partner. You do not want to attract attention as you leave, so go leave in the evening when there is no one to ask questions. Presumably, everyone else will be locked away in their homes, hoping to ride out Stage 2, hoping that it will just pass, but there is no such thing. Stage 2 leaps to Stage 3 in an aggressive manner, and then those folks disappear from existence. Do not stop unless you need gas or supplies. Take turns driving and sleeping with the person that is with you, so that you get to your destination quickly.

Escape by Foot

At some point, you will find yourself on foot. If you get a late start, or Stage 3 arrives quicker than you imagined, you might come across abandoned cars that block your path, there might be a blockade put together by the military, police, or looters. You might be ambushed, and your car is destroyed or your tires get punctured. You may make it to the region of your wilderness home, but the terrain is too shaky to continue, and the rest of the distance requires a hike. Whatever the case, there is not time to consider the options because there is only one: you grab your pre-packed backpack, you grab your weapons, and you remain mobile, continuing your journey by foot. This journey may begin in your neighborhood if your car is sabotaged or stolen, or on a highway if there are roadblocks that inhibit vehicular transportation. Be prepared for any scenario.

Remember, you are faster than a zombie. A zombie is experiencing rigor mortis and rotting flesh, and you are agile and quick. Their only chance to harm you is if you stop. Move at night if there is moonlight, and keep moving. Do not use any light to guide you and do not smoke a cigarette of sort for it will attract attention. If it is impossible to see at night, and daylight travel is the only option, you must be more vigilant. Stay off the roads, though you will probably have to skirt them in order to move quickly. The presumption is that you are traveling by foot because driving isn't possible because of obstacles, so there shouldn't be any vehicles on the road. When you do see a vehicle, you should be close enough to a wooded area to duck for cover. Avoid wide, open areas, and go around big cities that are between you and your final destination. This will take a considerable amount of time in some cases, but you cannot afford to trek through cities of any size. If it isn't an option to avoid them, stay on international highways, and never descend into the middle of a town, no matter how tempting. Try to move at night, during the dawn. Move quietly and take your time.

Once you reach the wilderness, do the same using animal paths and easy routes, to avoid having to trample through bushes and cut down vegetation with your machete. You want to stay invisible, but more importantly you want to move with stealth. Noise brings problems to you.

Traveling with a partner or a small team is crucial. It allows for one person to always be on guard whenever rest is needed. The entire team should not be asleep at the same time. At least one guard, preferably two, should be monitoring for approaching zombies and looters, using binoculars or night vision goggles for early detection. Breaks should be short, even for sleeping, but when you do sleep, do it during the day, and camouflage yourself and your gear with surrounding vegetation. Whisper and use visual signals.

Weapons should be at the ready: locked, loaded, and off of safety. Listen for the moans of the undead. Listen for vehicles of crooks and other criminals. Look for any movement, silhouettes, and shadows. You do not attack immediately. Avoid contact at all costs because you are only on the defensive. You hold your position and remain quiet and camouflaged in the hopes that any danger will pass without noticing you.

Defending Yourself

You are going to have to fight. No matter how fast you move, how quiet your group proceeds, or how camouflaged your position, you will have to bear arms and kill to survive. Get used to the idea now. You will become a warrior who will deal deadly blows as they are necessary for your survival. Any confrontation will cause a disturbance, and the possibility that more zombies arrive is great. You must "stick" and move.

Have a hand weapon in case of a sneak attack, which doesn't give you the proper space and time to pull a gun. Use a crossbow if a single zombie is near and heading in your direction in order to reduce the noise of the killing. Use your shotgun for a group of zombies that stumbles upon your location. You will not have time to reload bolts into your crossbow in that situation.

Moreover, always aim for the head. Hitting them somewhere else will temporally disable a zombie, which could allow for your escape, but its better to shoot them through their brains, and send them to their permanent end, never to be dealt with again.

During the entirety of your days inside of a zombie apocalypse, you do not go on the offensive. You attack only to defend yourself, your team, and your position. It might be tempting to search and kill zombies, but you will spend ammunition that you might need in the coming years, and you put yourself in danger of injury, death, or zombification. Your best bet to survive the apocalypse is to ride it out. The infection will die, the zombies will rot, and you will be able to rebuild a new world, free of zombies, and filled with the strongest and smartest of humans.

Congratulations, you made it through Stage 1 and 2 of the zombie apocalypse.

Section 4:

The Apocalyptic World

Stage 3: Settlement

After trekking through the wilderness, and arriving at your pre-scouted new home away from the world, a clandestine area in which contact with any human or zombie should be rare, you can take a deep breath, maybe even take a nap, but do not let your defenses down. In fact, you should begin fortifying your new abode for long-term protection and survival, as the world eats itself alive.

Defending Your Wilderness Home

If your vehicle made it into the woods, and was left behind as rough terrain made it impossible for it to move forward, park it in a camouflaged location. You will not be able to carry all of your additional supplies with you at one time, so several troops from the car will be necessary. Once you have all of your supplies begin building a fortified home. You wall want to build a cabin out of the wood that surrounds you on a place where visibility is optimal for spotting zombies and bandits. The fortified home should have small peepholes built for viewing and for rifles, but small enough that no person, dead or alive, can get through them. In other words, you should be able to fight off a hoard of zombies with your weaponry without one of them ever being able to penetrate your cabin. Once a fortified home has been built, begin building a fence that is at least 10 feet high as a second measure of defense. It should be impenetrable.

An escape route should be established if all is lost, and your team becomes separated. The fall back position should be the team's vehicle if they are in range. If not, choose a natural formation of rocks, a river, a marked grove of trees, etc. Whatever it might be, everyone should know the location on day 1 of your arrival. A roving guard or a lookout from a high tree should always be vigilantly watching your surroundings, every day, every night, and every hour of every day and night. There is never a time when someone isn't on guard duty.

Do not use lights at night, and while fires can be used, they must be built behind a wall, so that they cannot be seen, and only at night. Do not build fires during the day, and extinguish any fire you make it night before daybreak. You do not want to send smoke signals to the surrounding area, attracting raiders and the walking dead.

While you are building your fortified home, your team should be planting crops, and digging a well within your confines. Nearby water sources should be irrigated if possible, or at least be easily accessible. Crossbow hunting and fishing teams should be established. Someone should always be casting a net for fish or hunting anything that moves from squirrels to moose, and everything in between. Stock up supplies of meat jerky, and forage for berries and other edible vegetation while hunting.

Stage 4: Waiting out the Storm

Stay put, for the curious become the dead. You may think it smart to send out a team to perform reconnaissance of the closest population center to see if life has returned to normal after six months or a year, but it is a terrible idea. The scent of a fresh human will send a population of surviving zombies into a frenzy, and they might follow the trail back to your location. Use short-wave radios to pick up communications from surviving colonies and find possible news reports from operational government agencies, but do not attempt to respond to anything you hear. It could be a trap.

There isn't a safe time to evacuate your position and reenter the world. Essentially, you should only leave the nest of your fortified home, when you no longer wish to be alive because it is good possibility you will die. Also, remember when you leave, you are jeopardizing the others on your team, so there is no return, and if you are captured, only a coward would give up their team to save their life. However, after a few years, you won't have to worry much about the existence of bandits. Their constant mobility and anarchist ways will devour them in time. They will either run out of resources or run into a zombie hoard. In the third year, only zombies will exist and uninfected humans like you, who have settled to survive, who live of the land, and are vigilant everyday.

After 10 years, human populations will begin to grow, zombie existence should be eradicated, and sending a scout might become practical. Your team member might find that zombies still exist, that nothing has survived, or they might stumble upon a colony of decent people, or a military force willing to help. But you can never be sure of their sincerity in a post-apocalyptic world. The scout might stumble upon a den of Mad Max-like marauders, who force the person to take them to your fortress, but it is unlikely. Although, really, the possibilities are endless at what one might find, and there is only one reason to ever leave you new establishment, and that is if you are unsatisfied with your existence, and are no longer afraid of death; then, your curiosity might find further hope or shatter it completely. Sound advice would be to enjoy the sanctity of the life around you, of the team that has become your family, of the simple pleasures of living off the land and respecting the environment that surrounds you and all that you have created and survived.

Conclusion

Thank you again for downloading this book!

I hope this book was able to help you prepare properly for the impending zombie apocalypse.

If you enjoyed this book, then I'd like to ask you for a favor, would you be kind enough to leave a review for this book on Amazon? It would be greatly appreciated!

Be safe out there. I will see you on the other side of the apocalypse.

Thank you and good luck!